Women in the Old Testament

STUDY GUIDE

Catherine Upchurch

LITTLE ROCK SCRIPTURE STUDY
Little Rock, Arkansas

THE LITURGICAL PRESS
Collegeville, Minnesota

DIOCESE OF LITTLE ROCK

2500 North Tyler Street • P.O. Box 7239 • Little Rock, Arkansas 72217 • (501) 664-0340 • Fax (501) 664-6304

Dear Friends in Christ,

The Bible comes to us as both a gift and an opportunity. It is a gift of God who loves us enough to communicate with us. The only way to enjoy the gift is to open and savor it. The Bible is also an opportunity to actually meet God who is present in the stories, teachings, people, and prayers that fill its pages.

I encourage you to open your Bibles in anticipation that God will do something good in your life. I encourage you to take advantage of the opportunity to meet God in prayer, study, and small-group discussion.

Little Rock Scripture Study offers materials that are simple to use, and a method that has been tested by time. The questions in this study guide will direct your study, help you to understand the passages you are reading, and challenge you to relate the Scriptures to your own life experiences.

Allow the Word of God to form you as a disciple of the Lord Jesus. Accept the challenge to be "transformed by the renewal of your mind" (Romans 12:2). Above all, receive God's Word as his gift, and act upon it.

Sincerely in Christ,

✠ J. Peter Sartain
Bishop of Little Rock

Sacred Scripture

"The Church has always venerated the divine Scriptures just as she venerates the body of the Lord, since from the table of both the word of God and of the body of Christ she unceasingly receives and offers to the faithful the bread of life, especially in the sacred liturgy. She has always regarded the Scriptures together with sacred tradition as the supreme rule of faith, and will ever do so. For, inspired by God and committed once and for all to writing, they impart the word of God himself without change, and make the voice of the Holy Spirit resound in the words of the prophets and apostles. Therefore, like the Christian religion itself, all the preaching of the Church must be nourished and ruled by sacred Scripture. For in the sacred books, the Father who is in heaven meets His children with great love and speaks with them; and the force and power in the word of God is so great that it remains the support and energy of the Church, the strength of faith for her sons, the food of the soul, the pure and perennial source of spiritual life."

Vatican II, Dogmatic Constitution on Divine Revelation, no. 21.

INTERPRETATION OF SACRED SCRIPTURE

"Since God speaks in sacred Scripture through men in human fashion, the interpreter of sacred Scripture, in order to see clearly what God wanted to communicate to us, should carefully investigate what meaning the sacred writers really intended, and what God wanted to manifest by means of their words.

"Those who search out the intention of the sacred writers must, among other things, have regard for 'literary forms.' For truth is proposed and expressed in a variety of ways, depending on whether a text is history of one kind or another, or whether its form is that of prophecy, poetry, or some other type of speech. The interpreter must investigate what meaning the sacred writer intended to express and actually expressed in particular circumstances as he used contemporary literary forms in accordance with the situation of his own time and culture. For the correct understanding of what the sacred author wanted to assert, due attention must be paid to the customary and characteristic styles of perceiving, speaking, and narrating which prevailed at the time of the sacred writer, and to the customs men normally followed in that period in their everyday dealings with one another."

Vatican II, Dogmatic Constitution on Divine Revelation, no. 12.

Instructions

MATERIALS FOR THE STUDY

This Study Guide: Women in the Old Testament

Bible: The New American Bible with Revised New Testament or The New Jerusalem Bible is recommended. Paraphrased editions are discouraged as they offer little if any help when facing difficult textual questions. Choose a Bible you feel free to write in or underline.

Commentary: *Women in the Old Testament* by Irene Nowell, O.S.B. (The Liturgical Press) is used with this study. The assigned pages are found at the beginning of each lesson.

ADDITIONAL MATERIALS

Bible Dictionary: *The Dictionary of the Bible* by John L. McKenzie (Simon & Schuster) is highly recommended as an additional reference.

Notebook: A notebook may be used for lecture notes and your personal reflections.

WEEKLY LESSONS

Lesson 1—Women of Israel's Beginnings
Lesson 2—More Women of Israel's Beginnings
Lesson 3—Women of Israel's Passover
Lesson 4—Women of Israel's Early Tribes
Lesson 5—More Women of Israel's Early Tribes
Lesson 6—Women of Israel's Monarchy

YOUR DAILY PERSONAL STUDY

The first step is prayer. Open your heart and mind to God. Reading Scripture is an opportunity to listen to God who loves you. Pray that the same Holy Spirit who guided the formation of Scripture will inspire you to correctly understand what you read and empower you to make what you read a part of your life.

The next step is commitment. Daily spiritual food is as necessary as food for the body. This study is divided into daily units. Schedule a regular time and place for your study, as free from distractions as possible. Allow about twenty minutes a day. Make it a daily appointment with God.

As you begin each lesson read the assigned chapters of Scripture found at the beginning of each lesson, the footnotes in your Bible, and then the indicated pages of the commentary. This preparation will give you an overview of the entire lesson and help you to appreciate the context of individual passages.

As you reflect on Scripture, ask yourself these four questions:

1. *What does the Scripture passage say?*
   Read the passage slowly and reflectively. Use your imagination to picture the scene or enter into it.

2. *What does the Scripture passage mean?*
   Read the footnotes and the commentary to help you understand what the sacred writers intended and what God wanted to communicate by means of their words.

3. *What does the Scripture passage mean to me?*
   Meditate on the passage. God's Word is living and powerful. What is God saying to you today? How does the Scripture passage apply to your life today?

4. *What am I going to do about it?*

Try to discover how God may be challenging you in this passage. An encounter with God contains a challenge to know God's will and follow it more closely in daily life.

THE QUESTIONS ASSIGNED FOR EACH DAY

Read the questions and references for each day. The questions are designed to help you listen to God's Word and to prepare you for the weekly small-group discussion.

Some of the questions can be answered briefly and objectively by referring to the Bible references and the commentary *(What does the passage say?)*. Some will lead you to a better understanding of how the Scriptures apply to the Church, sacraments, and society *(What does the passage mean?)*. Some questions will invite you to consider how God's Word challenges or supports you in your relationships with God and others *(What does the passage mean to me?)*. Finally, the questions will lead you to examine your actions in light of Scripture *(What am I going to do about it?)*.

Write your responses in this study guide or in a notebook to help you clarify and organize your thoughts and feelings.

THE WEEKLY SMALL-GROUP MEETING

The weekly small-group sharing is the heart of the Little Rock Scripture Study Program. Participants gather in small groups to share the results of praying, reading, and reflecting on Scripture and on the assigned questions. The goal of the discussion is for group members to be strengthened and nourished individually and as a community through sharing how God's Word speaks to them and affects their daily lives. The daily study questions will guide the discussion; it is not necessary to discuss all the questions.

All members share the responsibility of creating an atmosphere of loving support and trust in the group by respecting the opinions and experiences of others, and by affirming and encouraging one another. The simple shared prayer which begins and ends each small group meeting also helps create the open and trusting environment in which group members can share their faith deeply and grow in the study of God's Word.

A distinctive feature of this program is its emphasis on and trust in God's presence working in and through each member. Sharing responses to God's presence in the Word and in others can bring about remarkable growth and transformation.

THE WRAP-UP LECTURE

The lecture is designed to develop and clarify the themes of the lesson. It is not intended to form the basis for the group discussion. For this reason the lecture is always held at the end of the meeting. If several small groups meet at one time, the large group will gather together in a central location to listen to the lecture.

Lectures may be given by a local speaker. They are also available on audio- or video-cassette.

LESSON 1   Women of Israel's Beginnings

Gen 12:4-5, 10-20; 17:15-22; 18:1-15; 21:1-8; 16:1-16; 21:9-21
Women in the Old Testament, pages 3–20

Day 1

1. Make a quick list of ten important characters from the Old Testament. How many on your list are women? Are their stories easy or difficult for you to recall?

2. a) Describe one significant female role model in your life.
   b) What qualities make a person a good role model?

3. What do you hope to gain from your study of women in the Old Testament?

Day 2 — Sarah

4. In your imagination picture Sarah, especially as she journeyed across the desert (12:4-5)? What do you see?

5. What emotions do you feel when you read that Abraham lied about Sarah's identity to protect himself (12:13) and to grow prosperous (12:16)? (See 20:2, 11, 14-15.)

6. How does God protect Sarah (12:17-19)? (See 20:3-18.)

Day 3

7. Why is it significant that Sarai is renamed by God (17:15-16)? (See 32:23-29; John 1:40-42.)

8. a) What words would you use to describe Sarah's role in God's promise (17:19, 21; 18:9-14)?
   b) Describe a time when you were convinced that God could accomplish anything (18:14). (See Matt 19:26; Mark 9:20-24.)

9. How can we explain two stories announcing the birth of Sarah and Abraham's child (17:16-19; 18:1-15)?

Different traditions

Day 4

10. a) What does Sarah's laughter tell you about her personality and faith (21:6-7)? (See 18:11-15.)

    b) Have you ever laughed at how God was working in your life? Describe.

11. Why is it significant that the final mention of Sarah is related to the purchase of land (23:1-20)? (See 12:1, 7; 15:7; 17:8.)

12. God's promise (12:1-3; 15:5; 17:4-8) is usually remembered as the covenant with Abraham, rather than the covenant with Abraham and Sarah (21:1-2). Why do you suppose this is the case? (See 17:19; 18:14; Isa 51:2.)

Day 5 — Hagar

13. a) What reasons could Sarah and Abraham give for taking matters into their own hands to get the child God promised (16:2-4)?

    b) Recall a time when you tried to direct God's plan for your life. What did you learn? Did you learn it immediately? Gradually?

14. Why would the promise of descendants be so important in the ancient world (16:10)? And why so important for Hagar, a woman and a servant? (See 15:5; 17:20; Ps 89:4-5; Isa 44:3; 66:22.)

15. What are the differences between how Sarah sees Hagar and how God sees Hagar (16:1-16)?

Day 6

16. Was it necessary for Sarah to jealously guard her son's interests against Hagar and Ishmael (21:9-12, 14)?

17. How do you think the later history of God's people has affected the way Hagar is remembered? (See Rom 9:6-9; Gal 4:22-31.)

18. Do you relate more easily to Hagar or to Sarah? Why?

LESSON 2   More Women of Israel's Beginnings

Gen 24:10-33, 59-67; 25:19-26; 26:6-11; 27:5-13, 41-46;
29:9–30:24; 31:14-35; 34:1-7, 24-31; 35:8, 16-20; 38:6-30
Women in the Old Testament, pages 21–46

Day 1

1. What is one lesson you would like to remember from last week's discussion and lecture about Hagar and Sarah?

Rebekah

2. What inner qualities does Rebekah reveal by offering water to a thirsty stranger and his animals (24:16-20)?

3. Rebekah and her family seem convinced of God's action by the servant's story (24:28-58). When has another person's faith story been helpful or convincing for you?

Day 2

4. What similarities should we see between the stories of Sarah (Gen 15–21) and Rebekah (Gen 24–26)?

5. List some of the ways Rebekah manipulated her family to make God's word to her (25:23) come true. (See 27:1-45.)

6. What advice would you give to parents about how to avoid favoritism?

Day 3 — Leah and Rachel

7. How do you feel about Jacob being deceived (29:21-27)? (Recall Gen 27.)

8. How do you think Leah felt knowing she was "second choice" (Gen 29:16-18, 21-27)? Can you describe a personal experience like Leah's?

9. In the modern world it may be difficult to imagine two wives competing to produce children for their husband (29:31–30:24). What kinds of rivalries between siblings have the power to be destructive today?

Day 4

10. How do both Rachel and Leah view the way they were "given" in marriage (31:15)?

11. In what ways does Rachel demonstrate that she is a strong woman as indicated by her son's name (35:18)?

12. Which qualities in either Rachel or Leah could help you in your spiritual journey at this time in your life? Why?

Day 5 — The Maids

13. How do we know that Deborah may have played a significant role in Isaac and Rebekah's family (35:8)?

14. The children of Zilpah and Bilhah form four of Israel's twelve tribes. Why can we assume the two women were never valued in their own right? (See Gen 33:1-2; 35:22.)

15. Put yourself in the shoes of these female servants. How might the story of Jacob and his family be told differently from the perspective of these "minor" characters?

Day 6 — Dinah and Tamar

16. a) Do you think Dinah's family was genuinely concerned about her or more concerned about their family reputation (34:5-31)?

    b) If Dinah could speak for herself, what might she say?

17. How would a widow benefit from the levirate marriage law? (See Deut 25:5-10.)

18. In what ways is Tamar "more righteous" (38:26) than Judah (38:6-30)?

LESSON 3   Women of Israel's Passover

Exod 1:15-22; 2:1-10, 15-22; 4:19-20, 24-26; 15:20-21;
Num 12:1-16; 20:1; Micah 6:3-4
Women in the Old Testament, pages 47–58

Day 1

1. a) Who was your favorite female character from Israel's beginnings (found in the previous two lessons)?
   b) What key lesson did you learn from her story?

The Midwives: Shiprah and Puah

2. What motivated Pharaoh to order the destruction of innocent
baby boys (Exod 1:15, 16, 22)? (See 1:8-14.)

3. The midwives disobeyed Pharaoh's command because they
"feared God" (Exod 1:17). Describe a time when your relationship with God gave you the courage to make a difficult decision.

Day 2 — Moses' Mother and Pharaoh's Daughter

4. Pharaoh saw the river as a means to destroy life (Exod 1:22).
How did Moses' mother use the river (Exod 2:3)?

5. In what specific ways is Moses' mother like Noah? Abraham?
and God? (Exod 2:2-10.) (See Gen 1:31; 7:1-23; 12:10-20.)

6. Pharaoh's daughter defied her father's orders because she
was "moved with pity" (2:6).
   a) How does this Egyptian woman embody the qualities of
   God? (See Ps 72:13; Isa 54:8; 63:9; Mark 1:40-41.)
   b) When has pity moved you to act with compassion and justice?

Day 3

7. The initial stories of Exodus illustrate women working together to save Moses. Give examples of women cooperating
together to accomplish good in our society.

8. What kinds of characteristics and values might Moses have received from his natural mother/nursemaid? From his adopted
mother?

9. Who were important mother figures for you as you grew up?
What characteristics and values have these women passed
on to you?

Day 4 — Miriam

10. What can you learn about Moses' older sister from the way she approached the daughter of Pharaoh (Exod 2:7-8)?

11. What recent event in your life has made you feel like dancing and singing, as Miriam did after being delivered from Egypt (Exod 15:20-21)?

12. a) What is the role of the prophet in Israel? (See Ezek 3:17; Micah 3:8; 2 Pet 1:20-21.)

    b) In addition to Miriam (Exod 15:20), who are some of the women the Bible describes as prophets? What are their roles? (See Judg 4:4-9; 2 Kgs 22:14-20; Isa 8:1-3; Jer 1:9; Luke 2:22-24, 36-38; Acts 21:8-9.)

Day 5

13. a) How does Miriam understand her role among God's people (Num 12:1-2)? (See Mic 6:4.)

    b) How does Israel use the challenge of Miriam and Aaron to clarify the leadership role of Moses (Num 12:1-14)?

14. Why is Kadesh a significant place for Miriam's death and burial (Num 20:1)? (See Gen 16:13-14; 20:1; Num 20:1-13.)

15. What personal qualities do you admire in Miriam?

Day 6 — Zipporah

16. How is Zipporah, a foreigner, placed within the tradition of Israel's ancestors (Exod 2:15-22)? (See Gen 24:34-49; 29:1-14.)

17. Zipporah acts as a mediator between God and Moses and in the process saves his life (Exod 4:24-26).

    a) How is her role similar to that of Jesus? (See Rom 5:1-2; Eph 2:13.)

    b) Describe a time when someone was a mediator of God's presence to you.

LESSON 4 — Women of Israel's Early Tribes

Josh 2:1-21; 6:20-25; Judg 4:1-24; 5:1-31; 11:29-40;
13:1-25; 14:1-20; 15:1-8; 16:1-22
Women in the Old Testament, pages 59–83

Day 1

1. List some of the ways women helped achieve Israel's Exodus? (Recall last week's lesson.)

Rahab

2. a) In what ways does Rahab prove that her faith outweighs her reputation (Josh 2:1-21)?
   b) When have you been surprised to discover that a person's poor reputation was not the entire picture of his or her worth?

3. Why do you suppose the biblical writers recorded Rahab's occupation (Josh 6:25), and listed her as one of the few women in the genealogy of Jesus (Matt 1:5)?

Day 2 — Deborah and Jael

4. Describe the historical period that gave rise to the judges in Israel. (See Judg 2:6-23; 17:6.)

5. a) By what authority did Deborah announce a military plan and direct its military leader into battle (Judg 4:4-9)?
   b) Have you ever experienced in yourself or others the kind of certainty and confidence Deborah displays? Describe.

6. According to the poetic version of the battle, what forces contributed to Israel's victory (Judg 5:3-5, 13-18, 21-22)?

Day 3

7. a) What words would you use to describe Jael's treatment of Sisera (Judg 4:17-22; 5:24-27)?
   b) Do you usually associate these words with battle? with women?

8. Why is Jael praised as a hero in Israel, "blessed among women" (Judg 5:24)?

9. Deborah describes herself as "a mother in Israel" (Judg 5:7) and then sings of Sisera's mother watching for him to return from battle (Judg 5:28-30). How would you feel looking at this story through the eyes of mothers on opposite sides?

Day 4 — Jephthah's Daughter

10. a) What did Jephthah value more, his reputation as a man of his word or his daughter's life (Judg 11:30-39)?
    b) List some ways you can keep your values in proper order?

11. Jephthah bargained with the Lord for military power but seemed powerless to save his daughter (Judg 11:30, 35). When have you wanted something badly only to discover it was not what you needed after all?

12. Jephthah's daughter took time to mourn her virginity (Judg 11:37). What might generations of Israelite women have mourned about her (Judg 11:40)?

Day 5 — The Women Around Samson

13. List the elements in the story of Samson's birth that show his mother as a person of strong faith (Judg 13:2-24).

14. Samson's mother was entrusted with her son's special consecration to God (Judg 13:4-5, 13-14). When have you felt you were entrusted with another person's welfare? How did you feel?

15. What lessons can we learn about greed and domestic violence from the story of Samson's marriage to the Philistine woman (Judg 14:1–15:8)?

Day 6

16. Reflect on the connection between Samson's marriage and his eventual defeat of the Philistines. Do you agree with the writer's view that Samson's marriage had been "brought about by the Lord" (Judg 14:4)? Would his wife agree?

17. In what ways is Delilah a suitable match for Samson (Judg 16:4-22)?

18. In what ways is Delilah like Samson's silent and victimized wife?

LESSON 5 — More Women of Israel's Early Tribes

Book of Ruth; 1 Sam 1–2
Women in the Old Testament, pages 85–101

Day 1

1. As you continue to study women from the tribal period, what is one thing you would like to remember from last week's discussion or lecture?

Three Widows: Orpah, Naomi, and Ruth

2. How are the causes of migration today similar to the causes in the ancient world (Ruth 1:1, 6)? (See Gen 26:17-22; Exod 2:15; 3:7-8; 1 Sam 31:7.)

3. a) What was Israel's relationship with the Moabites (Ruth 1:1)? (See Deut 23:4-7; Judg 11:17-18.)
   b) How could this historical and cultural situation complicate the lives of Naomi, Ruth and Orpah?

Day 2

4. How do Orpah, Ruth and Naomi break the stereotype we sometimes have about mothers- and daughters-in-law (Ruth 1:7-18)?

5. Orpah and Ruth both struggle with how best to care for Naomi and themselves (Ruth 1:7-18). Has there been any area in your family life where you had to decide whether to "go back" or "travel on"?

6. What does the practice of gleaning tell you about Israel's attitude toward and responsibility for the poor (Ruth 2:1-18)? (See Lev 19:9-10; Deut 24:19-22.)

Day 3

7. What are some of the factors that led Ruth to follow Naomi's instructions at the threshing floor (Ruth 3:1-6)?

8. a) Why is Boaz attracted to Ruth (Ruth 3:10)? (See Ruth 2:11.)
   b) What qualities do you appreciate most in those who are closest to you?

9. What matters must Boaz settle with another male relative before marrying Ruth (Ruth 3:12-13; 4:1-6)? (See Lev 25:23-28; Deut 25:5-6.)

Day 4

10. The Book of Ruth illustrates how God cares for human needs through loving relationships. When have you experienced God's care in a relationship with someone?

11. Israel learned lasting lessons about covenant love from a foreign woman. What lessons have you learned from those different from yourself?

12. Reread Ruth's promise to Naomi in Ruth 1:16-17. How can this familiar passage help you to make a deeper commitment to God's people?

Day 5 — Hannah and Peninnah

13. What kinds of emotional responses does Hannah's barrenness cause in Hannah herself (1 Sam 1:1-8)? in her husband? in Peninnah?

14. Recall a time when you pleaded with God to change a situation that seemed hopeless (1 Sam 1:10-17). What difference did your prayer make?

15. a) What kinds of things happen when the Lord "remembers" (1 Sam 1:19)? (See Gen 8:1; 30:22-23; Exod 2:23-24; 6:5-6.)
    b) What deeds of the Lord in your personal life do you want to hold in your memory?
    c) What are some of the biblical truths God would want you to remember? (For example, see Deut 6:4-6; Isa 43:1-2; Mic 6:8; Matt 5:3-12, 16, 43-48; 6:19-21; 7:7-12; John 3:16; 1 Cor 13.)

Day 6

16. How do you think Hannah felt as she gave her son to the service of the Lord and left him with Eli (1 Sam 1:24-28)?

17. If you were to write a hymn of praise recounting God's actions in your life recently what would be your theme (1 Sam 2:1-10)? Why?

18. What example did Hannah give Samuel and her other children by the way she visited the shrine (1 Sam 2:18-21)?

LESSON 6   Women of Israel's Monarchy

1–2 Samuel passim*; 1–2 Kings passim
Women in the Old Testament, pages 103–129

Day 1

1. What did you learn over the past two weeks about the role of women in Israel's tribal period?

Michal

2. a) What seems to be Michal's primary interest (1 Sam 18:28; 19:11; 2 Sam 6:16-23)?
   b) Does anyone in the story care about her interests?

3. If Michal lived in today's world, what sources of support and help might she find?

Day 2 — Bathsheba

4. What defense did Bathsheba have against the advances of King David (2 Sam 11:4)?

5. a) In Jewish law, what consequence awaited those caught in adultery? (See Lev 20:10; Deut 22:22.)
   b) When have you seen the fear of being caught lead someone to heap sin upon sin as David did (2 Sam 11:6-17)?

6. In your opinion, what was David's worst transgression against Bathsheba (2 Sam 11:4-27)?

Day 3

7. Why are forgiveness and reconciliation important not only for the sinner but for those around the sinner (2 Sam 12:11-19)? (See Ps 51.)

8. Compare Bathsheba's request on behalf of her son (1 Kgs 1:11-34) to the request by the mother of James and John (Matt 20:20-27).

9. In the end, how does the story show that Bathsheba did not remain a victim (1 Kgs 1:11–2:20)?

*Passim = scattered passages

Day 4 — Tamar

10. a) What lessons does Amnon need to learn about the difference between love and lust (2 Sam 13:1-17)? (See John 13:34; 1 Cor 13:1-13; James 1:14-15.)

    b) What lessons could David learn about how to be a loving parent (2 Sam 13:21)?

11. Which parts of the story of Tamar indicate that she was fighting to maintain her dignity in spite of the crime against her (2 Sam 13:7-20)?

12. In our world today what attitudes still need to change about rape and incest?

Day 5 — Queen of Sheba

13. How did the Queen of Sheba use her power and position (1 Kgs 10:1-2, 10-13)?

14. A foreign queen recognized Solomon's wisdom and leadership as gifts from the Lord and signs of God's presence (1 Kgs 10:6-9). Describe how someone has helped you to recognize the gifts and talents God has given you. (See Jas 1:16-17.)

15. The Queen of Sheba could have had the motto, "seeing is believing" (1 Kgs 10:7). What is your motto when it comes to learning? (See John 20:29.)

Day 6 — Jezebel

16. How did Jezebel use her power and position (1 Kgs 18:4; 19:2; 21:7-15)?

17. How might the telling of Jezebel's story have been affected by her status as a Phoenician (1 Kgs 16:31)? And as a woman?

18. a) What can be learned from Jezebel's story about Israel's struggle to obey the first commandment given centuries earlier at Sinai? (See Exod 20:2-6; Josh 24:14-15; Judg 10:6-16; 1 Sam 7:3-4; 2 Kgs 17:6-18.)

    b) What are some of the idols and false gods we sometimes worship today? (See 1 Cor 10:14; Gal 4:8-9.)

LESSON 7 Woman, Image of God

Gen 1:26-31; 2:21–3:7; Prov 8:1-3, 22-31; 9:1-5; 31:10-31;
Sir 24:1-27; 51:13-30; Wis 7:22–8:1
Women in the Old Testament, pages 131–151

Day 1

1. What new insight did you gain from last week's discussion or lecture?

The Genesis Ideal

2. a) What personal experiences have helped you believe you are an image of God (Gen 1:26-27)? (See Ps 8:5-6; Wis 2:23; Sir 17:1.)

   b) When has it been hard for you to believe this?

3. In what ways can we help our Church and society recognize and celebrate the image of God in both women and men?

Day 2 — Eve

4. a) How does a knowledge of the Hebrew words in Genesis 2:21-23 enhance your understanding of this second creation account?

   b) How might our cultural biases (or setting) affect the way we interpret such passages? (See 1 Cor 11:8; 1 Tim 2:13.)

5. In Genesis 2:23, the man expressed delight in his partner. What relationship in your life has recently been a source of delight in your life? Why?

6. In what ways does the Bible use the physical and emotional union in marriage as a teaching tool (Gen 2:24)? (See Isa 54:5; Matt 19:4-6; Eph 5:25.)

Day 3

7. Do you ever find yourself wishing we had remained in the garden, unaware of the difference between good and evil (Gen 2:17; 3:5)? In your experience, what responsibility comes with such knowledge? (See Deut 30:19-20.)

8. Eve and Adam are created as partners (Gen 2:18). Are they partners in crime and in punishment (Gen 3:1-7, 9-13, 16-19)?

9. Think of a time when you were tempted to make a bad choice. What or who prevented you?

Day 4 — Wisdom (Sophia)

10. In your experience has wisdom been easy to find (Prov 8:1-3)? Why or why not? (See Prov 1:20-21; 9:3.)

11. What evidence do you see in the created world that Wisdom was God's instrument of creation (Prov 8:22-31)? (See Ps 104:24; Rom 1:20.)

12. a) Do you recognize yourself among those invited to Wisdom's banquet (Prov 9:1-4)?
    b) What are some of the spiritual foods found at the table prepared by Wisdom (Prov 9:2, 5)? And what would be found at Folly's table (Prov 9:13-18)? (See Prov 12:16; 13:16; 14:29; 26:11; Eccl 2:13-14; 7:25.)

Day 5

13. What is an appropriate understanding of "fear of the Lord" (Prov 1:7; 9:10)? (See 1 Sam 12:24-25; Ps 130:4; Prov 8:13; 14:27; Jer 10:7; Rev 14:7.)

14. a) What skills and qualities make Wisdom a "worthy wife" (Prov 31:10), a woman of excellence (Prov 31:29)?
    b) List some of the "works" people see you do. What do these works tell people about your character (Prov 31:31)? (See Matt 5:16.)

15. a) Why does the author compare Wisdom to trees of the region or to flowing water (Sir 24:12-18, 23-27)?
    b) When has studying God's Word left you hungry and thirsty for more (Sir 24:20-22)? What have you done about it?

Day 6

16. To what extent has your own pursuit of wisdom matched your pursuit of love or success (Sir 51:13-30)? Have you noticed changes in different periods of your life? (See Ps 49:21; Prov 8:11; 16:16.)

17. Review the characteristics of Wisdom listed in Wis 7:22-24. Which of her characteristics has "permeated" your life and helped you be a mirror of God in your family or workplace (Wis 7:26)? (See Jas 3:13-18.)

18. What difference can it make in your prayer life that God's wisdom is described as a feminine image?

LESSON 8   Women of Courage and Strength

Jdt 8–16; Dan 13
Women in the Old Testament, pages 153–183

Day 1

1. What did you learn in last week's discussion and lecture that was most helpful in broadening your understanding of God?

Judith

2. What is the author of Judith suggesting by confusing the historical setting of Israel and its enemies?

3. In what ways does Judith "break the mold" of widows in the ancient world (Jdt 8:4-8)? (See Deut 24:17-18; 2 Kgs 4:1-7; Isa 10:1-2.)

Day 2

4. How does Judith's faith in God differ from the faith of the town's elders (Jdt 8:11-27)? (See Jdt 7:19-32.)

5. Uzziah proclaims that Judith has good sense and is wise, prudent and God-fearing (Jdt 8:28-31). Who are some of the others described like this? (See Exod 1:17; 1 Kgs 3:12; Job 1:1; Isa 11:2; Acts 7:9-10.)

6. a) How do you feel when you read the prayer Judith voices against her enemies (Jdt 9:7-14)? (See Ps 17:10-15; 58:4-12; 59:10-18.)

   b) What have you experienced that convinces you of the truth found in Judith 9:11? (See Ps 33:16-22; 86:1-17.)

Day 3

7. What do you believe was Judith's strongest weapon against Holofernes (Jdt 10:1–13:10)?

8. Why did Holofernes underestimate Judith's strength (Jdt 12:10-12, 16-20)?

9. Judith credits the defeat of Holofernes to divine power and human planning (Jdt 13:4-5). When have you felt God's power working through your plans?

Day 4

10. In what sense could Judith's act be considered a "deed of hope" (Jdt 13:19)?

11. How can the fruits of Judith's life help you appreciate her victory over Holofernes (Jdt 8:1-8; 16:21-25)? (See Luke 6:43-45.)

12. The story of Judith is filled with repeated references to her status as a woman (Jdt 10:3-4, 19; 11:21; 12:11-12, 16; 13:15; 14:18; 15:12-13.)

    a) Why is her gender important to the story?
    b) What positive lessons could women today gain from her story?

Day 5 — Susanna

13. a) What seems to be the major difference between Susanna and the two judges (Dan 13:9, 23)?
    b) How do you nourish a healthy conscience? (See 1 Tim 1:5; Heb 10:21-22; 1 John 3:21-24.)

14. What kind of power do the two men use against Susanna (Dan 13:20-27)? (See Lev 20:10; Deut 17:6; 19:15; 22:22-23; 2 Cor 13:1.)

15. Have you ever been falsely accused of something? What did you do? What did you learn about yourself in that situation?

Day 6

16. The people wrongly believed the elders were credible because of their status in the community (Dan 13:41). How do you determine a person's credibility?

17. Describe a time when you needed the courage of young Daniel to go against the crowd and stand up for justice or right (Dan 13:44-48)?

18. What situation in your life has called forth in you the kind of faith and trust seen in Susanna?

LESSON 9   Queen Esther

Book of Esther
Women in the Old Testament, pages 185–205

Day 1

1. In the last lesson, did you relate better to Judith or Susanna? Why?

Queen Esther

2. According to the king's male officials, what is the real problem presented by Queen Vashti (Esth 1:17-20)?

3. a) How do feel about the king's response to Vashti (Esth 1:19-22)?

   b) In what areas have you especially noticed that men's and women's roles are still changing? How have you responded?

Day 2

4. Try to put yourself in the position of Esther, a young exile called to meet and please the king (Esth 2:1-4, 8-9). How would you feel? Honored? Frightened? Used?

5. Why is it significant that Esther found honor and received the devotion of those in power (Esth 2:9, 15, 17)?

6. Has there ever been a time when you either hid your connections (Esth 2:10, 20) or took advantage of your connections (Esth 4:8; B:8-9)? What were the circumstances?

Day 3

7. How did Mordecai convince Esther to risk challenging the law (Esth 4:10-16)?

8. Have you ever chosen to fast during a crisis (Esth 4:16)? How did it affect you or the situation that concerned you? (See Isa 58:5-12; Joel 2:12-13; Matt 6:16-18.)

9. What is added to the story by the Greek additions in Esth C and D?

Day 4

10. a) If you were granted one request what would it be? Use your imagination.
    b) What conclusions can you draw about Esther based on her one request of the king (Esth 7:3)?

11. a) Esther named the oppressor of her people (Esth 7:6). Was this an act of vengeance or an act of justice?
    b) Who or what are the "Hamans" that threaten your parish community or family? Think of specific examples.

12. How can we be sure Esther's request was not purely one of self-interest (Esth 8:1-8, 11-12)?

Day 5

13. What is celebrated in the festival of Purim (Esth 9:22-32; F:4-10)?

14. Compare Queen Esther with her predecessor, Queen Vashti.

15. If Esther was alive today, what wrongs could she right? In what ways could she be a role model? (See Esth 4:14.)

Day 6 — Wrapping Up

Make time in your group to thoroughly discuss your responses to the following questions.

16. Throughout this study of women in the Old Testament, who has been your favorite? Why? Whose story was most challenging to you personally? Why?

17. What surprised you most about the women in the Old Testament?

18. If you had to select one woman's story to tell young girls as they grow up in our world and Church today, whose story would it be? What message would you emphasize?

NOTES